T0159884

Published by Ice House Books

Written and edited by Kayla Clibborn
Illustrated and designed by Sophie Willcox

Ice House Books is an imprint of Half Moon Bay Limited
The Ice House, 124 Walcot Street, Bath, BA1 5BG
www.icehousebooks.co.uk

ISBN 978-1-912867-44-8

Printed in China

Written by Kayla Clibborn

Illustrated by Sophie Willcox

Okay, folks, let's not beat around the bush.
This lovely little rock we live on? It's in crisis.
And it's kind of (definitely) our fault.
We humans are wonderful, innovative, creative little beings, but damn, we sure know how to make a mess of things. From unimaginable amounts of plastic floating in the ocean to heartbreaking deforestation levels – the hard facts are pretty scary. But amidst all the science and the fear and the guilt, there's one very important fact to remember: there's still hope. And luckily for us, the first step towards making a difference couldn't be more simple ...

GET INFORMED

IT'S A HOT MESS

When someone mentions global warming, do you find yourself asking these kinds of questions?

Um ... the temperature changes constantly – that's literally what seasons are. Who cares about a few degrees?

Last night I had to wear six jumpers and two pairs of socks to bed. Where's all this 'global warming' when you need it then, eh?

Fear not, climate-confused comrade! You're certainly not alone in finding it difficult to comprehend that the Earth is heating up when you're shovelling snow from your driveway. So, what on Earth does it all mean?

GLOBAL WARMING

Refers to the rise in the Earth's average surface temperature.

IT'S CAUSED BY ...

An increase in the amount of heat-trapping or 'greenhouse' gases in the atmosphere. This is a result of human activity including burning fossil fuels, deforestation, agriculture and excessive waste.

BUT IT'S COLD HERE!

Sudden cold snaps don't mean the scientists have got it wrong. As global warming occurs, the Arctic heats up, disrupting the polar weather patterns. This sends cold air further south, creating extreme cold weather in parts of the US and UK.

WHAT'S WRONG WITH A BIT O' WARM WEATHER?

Global warming will have a much greater impact than hotter summers. Rising sea levels will threaten heavily populated coastlines and weather in general will become more unpredictable and extreme, with longer droughts, worse wildfires and more intense cyclones and storms.

SO WASTED

When you throw something away, does it just disappear? Does your bag of unworn dresses get shot into space to the delight of fashion-forward aliens? Well, probably not. So where does it go? Landfill.

The average person in the UK produces more than 400kgs of waste per year.

Clothes contribute more than 92 million tonnes of waste to landfill every year.

Every year, roughly one third of all food produced globally for human consumption is wasted.

Landfills produce greenhouse gases and emit toxic substances that pollute soil and waterways.

How long will the stuff in our overflowing landfills take to break down?
2 MONTHS
30 YEARS
1 MILLION YEARS
50 YEARS
UP TO 200 YEARS
450 YEARS

THE THING ABOUT PLASTIC...

Psst! We have a bit of a plastic problem. It's just about everywhere, in just about everything. And since 91 per cent of it doesn't make it to the recycling bin, we are, quite literally, drowning in the stuff.

Virtually every piece of plastic ever produced (that's a whopping 8.3 billion tonnes) still exists on the planet in some form.

A floating mass of garbage known as the Great Pacific Garbage Patch occupies an area of the Pacific Ocean that's three times the size of France.

It's estimated that over 13,000 pieces of plastic litter are floating on every square kilometre of ocean surface.

Half of all plastic material ever produced has been made in the last two decades alone.

One million plastic bottles are bought around the world every minute.

More than half the world's sea turtles and 90 per cent of sea birds are regularly consuming plastic.

ANIMAL S.O.S.

Who are some of the biggest victims of a warming planet, oceans full of plastic and humans' pesky penchant to over-consume? The precious and adorable creatures that we've come to know and love via David Attenborough's soothing voice.

In the past 40 years, there's been a 60 per cent decline in the general populations of all mammals, birds, fish, reptiles and amphibians.

Habitat destruction and overuse of pesticides has contributed to a huge decline in honey bee colonies around the world.

Due to shrinking sea ice, Adelie penguin populations have reduced by almost half and polar bear numbers are predicted to decline.

Orangutans have lost more than 80 per cent of their natural forest habitat as a result of palm oil and timber plantations.

POLLUTED PLANET

We often dismiss pollution as the fault of big, nasty corporations with maniacal overlords plotting the planet's demise from their skyscraper lairs. And while big business sure has a lot to answer for, there are a lot of habits that we regular folk could do with changing, too.

Transport is the largest source of greenhouse gas emissions in the UK. Seven million car journeys are made daily in London alone, and two million of those are under two kilometres

Every day, humans use more than a million terajoules of energy. That's the equivalent of every person on Earth – all 7 billion of us – each boiling 70 ettles every hour for 24 hours!

Petroleum-based chemicals from household products like cleaners, perfume and paint contribute as much to air pollution as vehicles do.

Chemicals and microplastics from cosmetics and soaps are washed down drains daily. More than 80 per cent of the world's wastewater is released into the nvironment without treatment.

DON'T PANIC!

Right – that was a whole lot of scary information! Before you go hiding under the bed in fear, redirect your wide-eyed horror towards the lovely words of encouragement belo

THE TIME TO ACT IS NOW. IT'S NOT TOO LATE! YOUR ACTIONS ARE MORE POWERFUL THAN YOU THINK.

CHANGING YOUR HABITS IS EASIER THAN IT LOOKS. PROMISE!
YOUR CONTRIBUTION WILL HELP HEAL OUR LOVELY LITTLE PLANET AND PROTECT THE RAD BEINGS THAT CALL IT HOME.
MAKING SUSTAINABLE CHOICES WON'T COST YOU AN ARM AND A LEG.

The term 'sustainability' gets thrown around a lot these days. So, what does it actually mean? Sustainability, put simply, means avoiding environmentally harmful practices now, in order to maintain ecological balance for the future. Taking that extra moment to stop and think about what you're buying, using, wasting and consuming can make a huge difference to your environmental footprint. Do you really need three plastic-wrapped peppers, or will two loose ones be enough? Should you drive to the shops, or could you walk instead? Ask yourself these questions and voilà! You can ...

THINK SUSTAINABLY

BEE-AUTIFUL!

THE WHOLE PACKAGE

Your plastic-free revolution starts at the supermarket. Let's go on a journey from trolley to shelf, to see where you can make a difference from your ingredients to your leftovers.

BEE RESPONSIBLE!

JUST SAY NO

Choose cloth or calico bags over plastic and reuse any plastic bags you do have. Remember to keep a few bags in your backpack, briefcase or handbag for those spontaneous shopping trips.

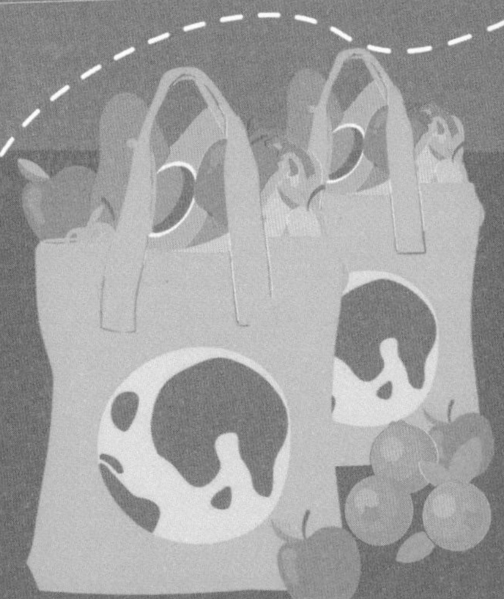

GET LOOSE

Only need two carrots, but there's a foam tray with three for the same price? These deals seem like a bargain, but they're costing you more in wasted food and unnecessary packaging. Choose loose produce and buy only what you need.

CONTAIN YOURSELF

Having chicken for dinner? Whipping up a cheese platter? Head to the deli counter to avoid the packaging. Enquire at your local supermarket about bringing your own reusable containers for deli items, so you can ditch the plastic and paper wrap, too.

WRAP IT UP

How much plastic film or foil do you use to keep your leftovers fresh? Switch to resuable cotton food wraps coated with beeswax or plant-based wax. They're totally compostable and come printed with cute patterns to keep your fridge lookin' fresh.

WHAT A LOAD OF RUBBISH

Plastic takeaway containers make handy ...

- food containers for leftovers
- lunchboxes
- pet water bowls
- pantry storage dishes

Plastic bottles make nifty ...

- watering cans
- herb planters
- kids' pencil holders
- bird feeders

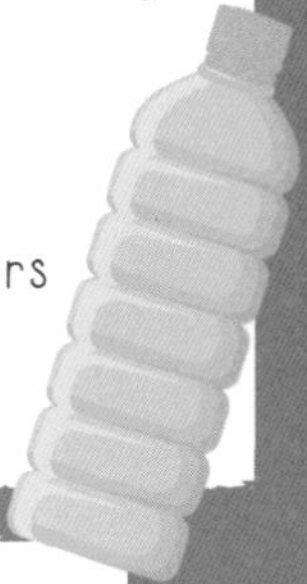

Tin cans make excellent ...

- desk organisers
- toothbrush holders
- mini plant pots
- garden lanterns

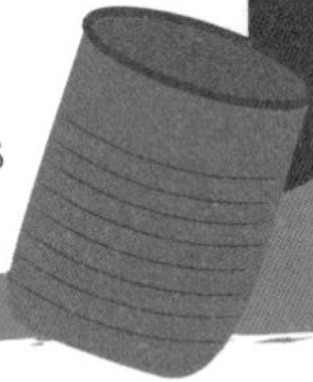

Glass jars make lovely ...

- containers for spices, nuts and cereals
- mini flower vases
- drinking glasses
- decorative light or candle holders

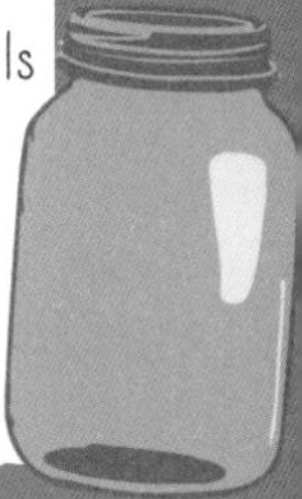

Composted food waste enriches soil and reduces methane emissions. You don't need a green thumb to make use of your food scraps – just keep it simple.

- Keep a separate bin with a tight-fitting lid for things like vegetable peels, citrus rinds, eggshells and coffee grounds.
- Don't add things like fish, meat, dairy products, grease or oil.
- Dig a hole in the garden about 30cm deep, add the compost and cover it up.

WE GET AROUND

Unless you live in some kind of peaceful, vehicle-free oasis, you only need to walk outside to see the number of cars cluttering the roads. Ditching the car for more eco-friendly transport options often means huge benefits for your health and your wallet.

TAKE A WALK

Walking is excellent exercise and, obviously, absolutely free. Think twice before taking the car for short, perfectly walkable journeys.

ON YOUR BIKE

Cycling is even better exercise, while providing zero-emission speed and efficiency. Bicycles also, on average, cost a fraction of the price of buying, maintaining and running a car.

HITCH A RIDE

Car-pooling and ride-share services ensure that a car is being used in the most efficient way possible. Do a little research and you're likely to find a ride-share option in your area for your morning commute, trip to the coast or Friday night taxi home.

GO PUBLIC

Hopping on the bus, train, tram or ferry leaves a far smaller footprint than driving. Not only are you removing your own car from the road, but every other commuter beside you is doing the same.

BEE
CAREFUL!

BRIGHT IDEA

There's more to energy efficiency than just turning off the telly when *Game of Thrones* is finished. There are a few extra things you can do to improve your energy consumption at home, reduce your carbon footprint and lower the cost of those bills, bills, bills, too.

Switch off appliances on standby mode.

Choose appliances with high energy ratings.

Heat only the areas of your home that need heating.

Switch to energy-efficient light bulbs.

Run your washing machine with cold water instead of hot.

Only fill the kettle with the amount of water you need.

If you have a thermostat, reduce the temperature by one degree Celsius.

Got the energy to go the extra mile?

Consider switching to a green energy supplier that uses renewable resources such as solar power, wind power or hydroelectricity.

EVERY LAST DROP

It can be hard to fathom the need to save water when you're watching the rain drizzle down the kitchen window. But using water more efficiently doesn't only prevent waste – it also lowers greenhouse gas emissions, as it takes loads of energy to purify, heat and distribute water to households. Making tiny changes to your habits can make a huge difference to your water usage.

Got a leak? Fix it! A tap that drips 45 times per minute wastes the equivalent of 10 baths per year.

Brushing your teeth? Peeling vegetables? TURN OFF THAT TAP!

Spruce-up your shower with low-flow, water-saving shower heads.

As much as you love your house plants, they don't need drinking water. Catch rainwater and use that to water your plants instead.

While your shower singing is surely divine, try capping those solos at a radio-worthy five minutes.

If you are dishwasher-blessed, only run it when you have a full load.

I'M A BUBBLE-BEE!

GOODY TWO SHOES

There are so many excellent humans working away to conserve and preserve our planet. And guess what? You can be an excellent human, too! Consider how you can use your time (or your cash) to give back and do good.

BACK TO NATURE

Look for tree-planting events near you and spend your Sunday with nature rather than Netflix. Don't want to get your hands dirty? Get your boots dirty instead. Visit your local national parks and conservation areas, read the info and pay the recommended entry fee.

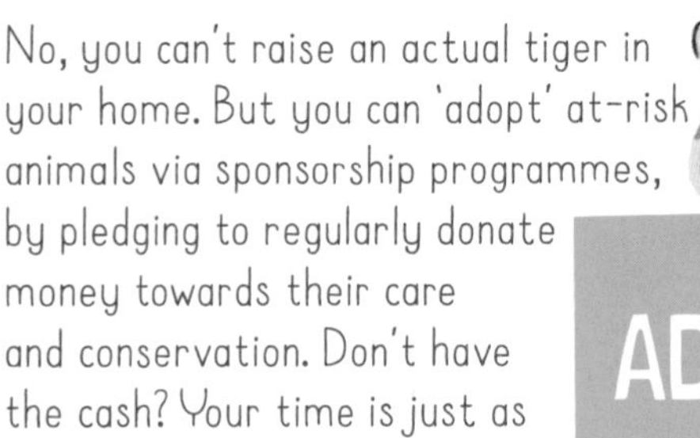

ADOPT ME

No, you can't raise an actual tiger in your home. But you can 'adopt' at-risk animals via sponsorship programmes, by pledging to regularly donate money towards their care and conservation. Don't have the cash? Your time is just as valuable. Consider volunteering at your local wildlife centre.

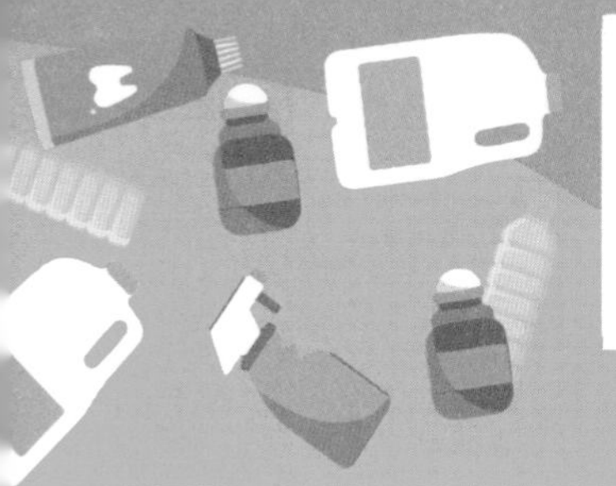

LOVE WHERE YOU LIVE

Bits of rubbish floating through your local park, or littering your street? Be a doll and bin 'em.

TAKE ME TO THE BEACH

Next time you head to the beach, take a bag with you and pick up any rubbish you see strewn across the sand.

Don't mind a spot of retail therapy? Don't worry, you're not alone. And you're not totally to blame, either. The temptation to spend, spend, spend smacks us in the face every time we leave the house: two-for-one deals, end-of-season sales, dachshund-shaped sofa cushions. You can probably guess why this is such a problem. Yep, that's right: excessive waste. Last season's coats, shoes and homewares are being used once, or not at all, replaced with a shiny new alternative and thrown away. It's time to put away our credit cards and learn to ...

BUY LESS STUFF

SECOND-HAND, SECOND HOME

SWEET THREADS

Demand for donated clothes in developing nations is declining as they opt to make their own textiles, meaning tonnes of clothes go to waste. So, chucking your bag of never-worn shirts into the charity bin doesn't quite cut it. Think twice before retiring something from your wardrobe and consider these alternatives

DONATE TO A MATE

Regret acquiring such a hefty collection of Hawaiian shirts? Don't forget that one person's fashion mistakes are another's fashion wins. Before you ditch something, ask your friends or family if they'd like it first.

SWAP IT OUT

Rather than guiltily eyeing your pile of unwanted clothes and shoes every time you pass it, try hosting a clothes swap. Invite your mates and their unwanted wares, crack a few beers, pour a little wine and get swapping!

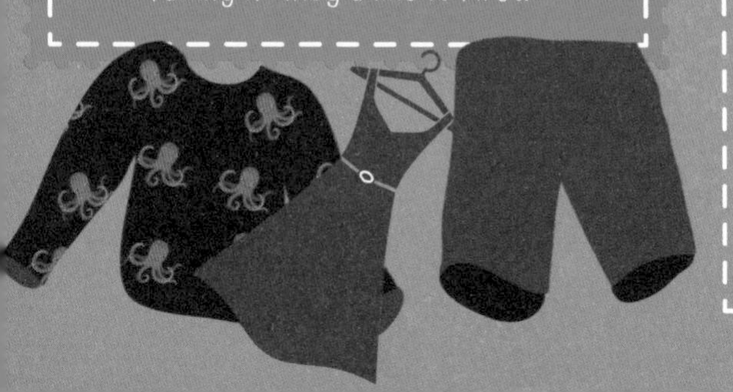

UPCYCLE AWAY

So no one wants your bright-orange T-shirt and – let's be honest – fair enough. But would a few alterations transform it into a cute headscarf? A nifty shopping bag? Is it a little faded? Dye it! Feeling a little '60s? Tie-dye it!

PATCH IT UP

A hole doesn't always mean a jacket has seen its last winter. Grab a needle and thread and sew that so-and-so up. If mending clothes and shoes is a bit beyond your skillset, head to your local tailor or cobbler and pay a few bucks to get them fixed. If your holey top is a little holey-er than thou, use it as a cleaning cloth.

IN THE BAG

You might have read the previous page and thought, "how in Attenborough's name do I make a T-shirt into a shopping bag?" Grab your scissors and follow the easy-peasy instructions below.

YOU WILL NEED:

- An old T-shirt or vest top
- Sharp scissors
- Fabric marker pen

STEP 1:

Turn your shirt inside out and cut off the sleeves (if it has them).

STEP 2:

Cut around the neckline so that the shirt is an even depth front and back. This will form the opening of your bag.

STEP 3:

Decide how deep you'd like your bag to be and trace a line across the bottom. It should be at least four centimetres above the shirt's hem.

STEP 4:

Using your scissors, cut slits from the bottom of the shirt up to the line. Cut the front and back of the shirt together, so that all the strips are the same width (about one to two centimetres).

STEP 5:

Take the first pair of strips – one from the front, one from the back – and tie them in a knot. Do the same with two more pairs of strips.

STEP 6:

Take one strand from the middle pair of strips and tie it to one of the strands in the first pair. Tie the remaining strand to one of the strands in the third pair.

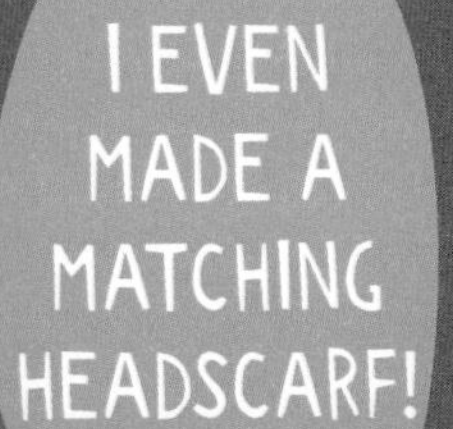

STEP 7:

Take the remaining strand from the third pair and tie it to the next set of strips.

STEP 8:

Repeat this process until all the strips are tied.

STEP 9:

Turn your bag back in the right way and marvel at the beauty of your upcycled creation.

LOVE LOCAL

Buying from local butchers, bakers and candlestick makers is not only a great way to support your local community, it can also reduce your environmental footprint. Small production means small emissions, so far fewer greenhouse gases have been used to deliver your meal to your plate or your socks to your feet.

YOUR LOCAL PLATE IS ...

FRESHER

LESS TRAVELLED

OFTEN ORGANIC

Less likely to be contaminated

FREE RANGE

Less wasteful

Great for the local economy

IN SEASON

MORE NUTRITIOUS

MORE SUSTAINABLE

More transparent: HOW WAS YOUR FOOD PRODUCED? Just ask!

YOUR LOCAL WARDROBE IS ...

LESS LIKELY TO USE SYNTHETIC FIBRES

Great for the local economy

NOT MASS PRODUCED

OFTEN MORE UNIQUE

Ethical – no sweat shops here

MADE FROM LOCALLY SOURCED MATERIALS

Better quality

LESS TRAVELLED

Less wasteful

YOUR CLUTTERED SHELF

Have you got several products in the cupboard that all do the same thing? Perform a little audit to see where you can smarten up and cut down.

WASHING UP LIQUID & ANTIBACTERIAL SPRAY

Antibacterial sprays kill the same number of germs as plain old soap and water. Just add washing up liquid to a wet cloth to wipe-up your wine spills.

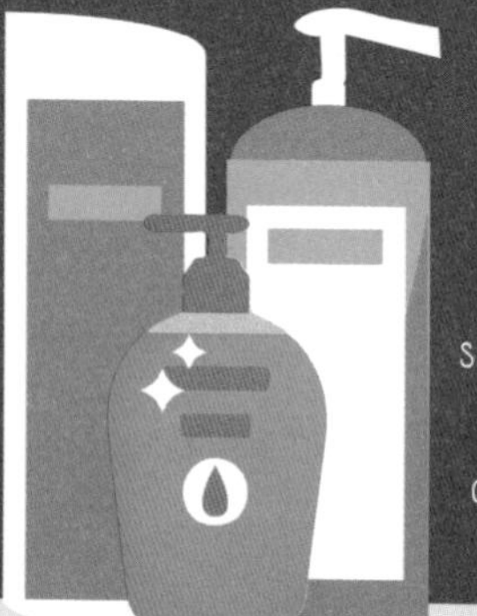

BODY WASH, SHAMPOO & CONDITIONE

Everyone's skin and hair is different and sometimes we need special stuff. But if you usually just grab any old product, consid switching to an all-in-one bar that triple acts as soap, shampoo and conditioner. You'll cut your three plastic bottles down to zer

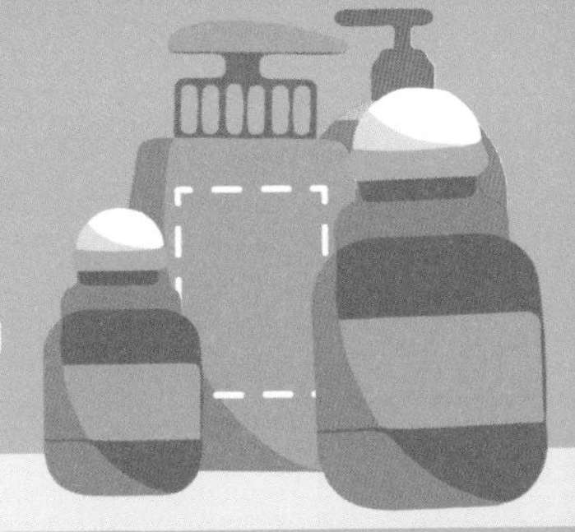

CLEANSER, TONER, MOISTURISER, SERUM, NIGHT CREAM, PRIMER....

Got a seven-step beauty routine? Eight steps? Ten steps? Consider how many different products (and plastic bottles) you really need and think twice before you re-stock.

MAKE-UP WIPES & FACE WASH

Make-up wipes are unrecyclable, un-flushable and unnecessary. Instead, use your face wash and a washable, reusable cloth to remove your make-up.

LIGHT 'EM UP

We all love to fill our homes with pretty little things, and a great place to find them is your local charity shop. But an even more eco-friendly way to adorn your mantel or your garden is to make it yourself! Follow these easy steps to make lovely, upcycled tin-can lanterns to (literally) brighten up your home.

YOU WILL NEED:

- Cleaned, empty tin cans (the kind that hold your instant coffee or chopped tomatoes)
- Hammer
- Nails
- Paper
- Pencil
- Masking tape
- Scissors
- Paint
- Tea light or votive candles

STEP 1:

First, remove the labels from your cans. You can do this by soaking them in hot water, then gently scrubbing them until all the adhesive is removed.

STEP 2:

Fill your cans with water and freeze overnight until solid. The ice helps give the can some resistance so that it doesn't get bent or crushed by the hammer and nail.

STEP 3:

Cut an A4 piece of paper in half length-ways, so it's wide and long enough to wrap around the can.

STEP 4:

Decide what picture or pattern you would like on your lanterns and draw it on the piece of paper. Make one of these for every can. The light from the candle will shine through the holes that make the outline of the pattern or shape.

STEP 5:

Wrap one piece of paper around each can and secure it with tape.

STEP 6:

Cradle the can on a folded towel. This will help stop the can from slipping and soak up any melted ice.

STEP 7:

Position a nail above the pattern or shape, and gently tap a few times with your hammer until the tip of the nail has punched the can. Repeat around the entire outline of your pattern or shape.

STEP 8:

Remove the paper and run the cans under warm water until the ice has melted.

STEP 9:

Paint the cans to your liking and let them dry.

STEP 10:

Once dry, add a tea light or votive candle inside each lantern and watch them glow!

COOL STUFF

While the intention of these last few pages was to encourage you to buy less, of course we're all human and sometimes we need stuff. Fortunately, there are many clever cookies creating amazing eco-friendly products for when you do need to hit the shops.

Treat your teeth to a bamboo toothbrush. They're recyclable, biodegradable and made from natural materials.

Ladies – rejoice! You can now replace your unrecyclable tampons and pads with a single, reusable menstrual cup that lasts for years.

Grab your very own metal or bamboo straw to keep in your bag for those smoothie emergencies.

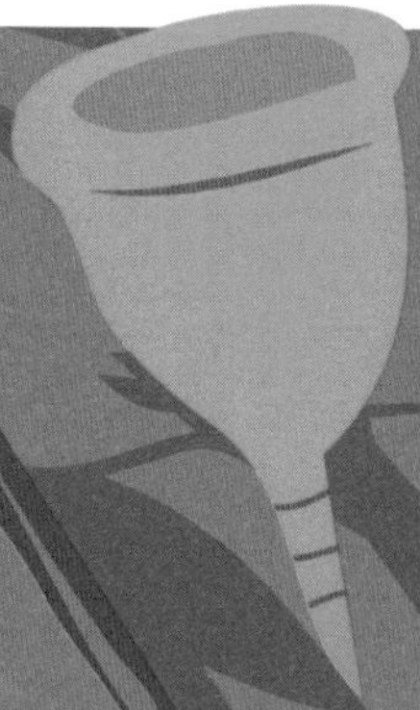

Reusable water bottles are not only far better than single-use plastic – they're also becoming kind of ... trendy! You can treat yourself to a pretty, floral pattern or a sleek, matte-black number. And to make them extra cool (literally), most are double-walled so they'll keep your water chilled for hours.

Caffeine addicts have their choice of reusable coffee cups made from bamboo, glass, stainless steel and even coffee bean and rice husks! To sweeten the deal, many cafés now offer a discount to those who bring their own cup.

Product labels can be scary things. They're often filled with long, impossible-to-pronounce words written in tiny, impossible-to-read text. But knowing the ingredients or materials used to make your shampoo, detergent, bronzer or cardigan can be a great way to empower you to make more eco-friendly choices. So next time you're at the supermarket, the boutique or the make-up counter, whip out your spectacles and ...

READ THE LABEL

IT'S CRUELTY FREE!
VEGAN 100%
CRUELTY FREE

MIRROR, MIRROR

It'd be a big job to assess every ingredient in every cosmetic product that you use. On top of that, most ingredients are long, scientific and scary-sounding anyway. Instead, keep an eye out for two common nasties: microplastics and siloxane.

ALL THAT GLITTERS

Brace yourselves, unicorns. Glitter, while magical, is made from harmful microplastics. These tiny particles are not retained by wastewater treatment and, when washed down the drain, end up in the ocean as a great threat to marine life. Avoid products that contain glitter and ditch the festival sparkles, too. Instead, check out one of the clever brands creating plant-based biodegradable glitter.

SMOOTH CRIMINAL

Siloxane is a chemical used in many cosmetics to make your skin soft and your hair silky smooth. But not only is siloxane toxic for marine life when washed down the drain, it also releases harmful emissions as it wears off your skin or hair throughout the day. Next time you're scanning your lotion label, keep your eyes peeled for any ingredient names ending in 'siloxane', and try to steer clear.

THESE MICROPLASTICS ARE NOT COOL.

SO FRESH, SO CLEAN

No one has the time or attention span to decipher every unintelligible word on the back of a bottle of kitchen spray. But, unfortunately, many cleaning products contain chemicals that are harmful to marine life when washed down the drain. So, how can you ensure you're using fish-friendly products? Make your own!

FOR GLASS AND WINDOWS

Grab an empty spray bottle (you know you've got a few under the sink) and fill it with half white vinegar, half water. It'll work like a dream when wiped with a soft rag or microfibre cloth.

FOR SURFACES AND SPILLS

Fill an empty spray bottle almost to the top with hot water. Add three tablespoons of white vinegar and two tablespoons of eco-friendly washing-up liquid, and shake well. Use this to clean counters, tables, tiles and bathrooms.

FOR THE TOUGH STUFF

Combine three tablespoons of baking soda with one tablespoon of eco-friendly washing-up liquid. Add warm water until it forms a paste and apply to a non-abrasive scouring pad. Use this to scrub toilets, bathtubs and sinks.

CRUEL AIN'T COOL

No animal should suffer just so that we can have bright-red lips or super silky skin. When buying cosmetics and household products, check the labels for the these three guarantees and start creating your cruelty-free cupboard.

BEE FRIENDLY

Give the bees something to buzz about and add a few daisies, marigolds or geraniums to your garden or windowsill. This encourages pollination and provides bees with extra habitat and food supply.

Look out for labels marked 'cruelty free' or 'not tested on animals'.

Orangutans have lost huge areas of their natural habitat as a result of unsustainable palm oil plantations. Palm oil is found in lots of products from shampoo to lipstick to detergent, so it can be hard to avoid. If you can't find products that are palm oil free (it's often listed as vegetable oil), look for products marked as using certified sustainable palm oil.

Look out for cosmetic and household products that are labelled vegan. This means the product not only avoids ingredients that have been tested on animals, but it excludes ingredients derived from animal products, too.

MATERIAL WORLD

It's true that buying more eco-friendly clothing is often not so wallet-friendly. The best thing to do (aside from buying second-hand) is to buy less. Owning fewer better-quality products is far cheaper and more sustainable in the long run than buying more, lower-quality products that only need replacing after a few wears. So, when you do hit the shops, spend a little extra time reading that T-shirt tag.

RESEARCH CLOTHING BRANDS THAT ...

- pay a fair wage to their workers
- offer return and recycle programmes to customers
- boast a 'fair trade' label

LOOK OUT FOR FABRICS THAT USE ...

- non-toxic, plant-based dyes
- recycled materials and fibres
- organic, biodegradable fibres

It's plant - based fashion!

LOOK FOR ECO-FRIENDLY FABRICS LIKE ...

- linen
- hemp
- bamboo

TRY TO AVOID SYNTHETIC OR HIGH-EMISSION FABRICS LIKE ...

- polyester
- non-organic cotton
- polyurethane (or PU)

COFFEE, COFFEE, COFFEE

How much do you know about the environmental cost of your cappuccino? Coffee production uses huge amounts of water and often requires large-scale deforestation (not to mention the disposable cups littering our landfills). But don't panic – you don't have to give up your morning cuppa. Simply paying a little more attention to your coffee habits will make a big difference.

DITCH THE DISPOSABLES

Popping by your local café? Say 'no' to the disposable takeaway cup and sit down, sip and savour. If you can't spare the time, invest in a reusable coffee cup to use on the go.

SEARCH FOR A STAMP OF APPROVAL

Check your coffee labels are marked 'certified organic', 'fair trade' or stamped with the Rainforest Alliance logo. This ensures your coffee is grown using sustainable farming practices. However, some small production roasters can't afford costly certification. So, if you've got a favourite brew, check the brand's website for details, contact them directly or ask your barista.

IMPROVE YOUR HOME BREW

How do you make your coffee at home? If you use an automated machine with plastic coffee pods or paper filters, consider switching to a plunger, stove-top moka pot or sniff out a quality instant coffee.

THE SUN WILL COME OUT TOMORROW

GET INFORMED

BUY SECOND-HAND

SAVE WATER

REUSE WHAT YOU HAVE

COMPOST YOUR FOOD SCRAPS

WALK, CYCLE, BUS, CAR-POOL

"Live like there's no tomorrow" is a lovely sentiment for a fridge magnet, but a pretty unsustainable rule to live by. There IS a tomorrow. There ARE consequences today. Tomorrow matters and it's our job to protect it.

REDUCE ENERGY USE

CHOOSE LESS PACKAGING

DO GOOD AND GIVE BACK

BUY LOCAL

CHOOSE CRUELTY FREE

READ THE LABEL